Sounds of Jazz

- **BOOK 1**

BOOK 2

by TONY CARAMIA

Commissioned by Frances Clark and Louise Goss

Edited by Louise Goss and Sam Holland

Preface

These piano compositions in jazz idiom were created so that student pianists can experience the joy of playing blues, rags and other jazz styles in a manner as authentic as possible within their rhythmic and technical capabilities.

The sounds of jazz are many and varied—from the raucous and rollicking ragtime/stride of Eubie Blake and Jellie Roll Morton, to the smooth and elegant swing of Teddy Wilson, to the unpredictable and daring bop of Thelonious Monk, to the ebullient and effervescent style of Chick Corea.

For the development of a true and natural jazz feel, the importance of listening cannot be overemphasized. Records, concerts and jam sessions are the real training ground for the ear. No amount of talk or written word can explain or take the place of hearing a jazz performance.

I hope these collections will supplement listening experiences with the excitement and satisfaction of actually performing jazz styles.

Tony Caramia

Tony Caramia is a nationally recognized jazz pianist, improvisational artist, composer and teacher. He earned Bachelor of Music and Master of Music degrees from the State University of New York (Fredonia) where he studied piano with Claudette Sorel and David Yeomans. Currently he serves as Assistant Professor of Group Piano Instruction and Jazz Piano Improvisation at the University of Illinois (Champaign-Urbana).

Mr. Caramia has performed widely as both classical and jazz artist. In 1979 he placed second in the World Championship Old-Time Piano Playing Contest at Monticello, Illinois and for the past several years has been invited to participate in the National Ragtime Festival in St. Louis. In 1982 he took part in the First International Symposium on Teaching Music for Children in West Berlin. He frequently appears as jazz clinician for colleges, universities and music teachers' organizations.

During the 1980-81 academic year, Mr. Caramia took a leave of absence from the University of Illinois to teach and compose at the New School for Music Study where these fresh and delightful compositions were created. We are proud to present the musical results of this happy collaboration.

Frances Clark

Louise Goss

Contents

4

Ragtime melodies have syncopation over a steady accompaniment. Make sure the left-hand is "march-like" and give the melodic syncopations a little extra weight.

The Kingston Rag

Driving along

6

Here's a "strut" made entirely of one pattern. Be sure to stress the "blues notes" (the lowered 3rd and 7th of each major scale).

Staccato Strut

Strut your stuff!

In this slow and gentle ballad, try for a flowing melody in the right hand with smooth harmonic changes in the accompaniment. Take your time in the last four measures.

Tender Night

Slowly and gently

Like most rags, this one is peppy and energetic. The audience should want to tap their feet, clap their hands or even dance! Always stress the syncopations:

Rag Man

Carefree, with bounce

This is a "blues" which uses a "walking" bass, moving stepwise up or down on every beat of the measure. Emphasize the 3rds and 7ths, especially when minor becomes major.

Slow-Walkin' Guy

With a steady, relaxed swing

Play this ballad in a lyrical manner, following carefully the contour and dynamic levels of the melody.

Ballad

Warmly singing

12

Not all ragtime needs dynamic contrast, but this one definitely does! Ragtime always has a quick snap in the accompaniment. In the last two lines imagine that you have a marching band behind you.

Ragged Romp

14

Notice that in this rag, the right hand plays almost all major and minor triads. Enjoy the syncopation created when the fourth beat is tied into the next measure!

Triadic Rag

What we call "the jazz sound" is often a mixture of major and minor thirds in an overall major context. The whole piece is made of the pattern introduced in measures 1 and 2; in line 5, the first four notes of the figure are turned upside down. Keep a steady tempo with even articulation.

The Scrambler